RECIPE

Serves: Prep time:

Ingredients:

Method:

RECIPE

Serves: Prep time:

Ingredients:

Method:

RECIPE

Serves: Prep time:

Ingredients:

Method:

RECIPE

Serves:

Prep time:

Ingredients:

Method:

RECIPE

Serves: Prep time:

Ingredients:

Method:

RECIPE

Serves: Prep time:

Ingredients:

Method:

RECIPE

Serves: Prep time:

Ingredients:

Method:

RECIPE

Serves: Prep time:

Ingredients:

Method:

RECIPE

Serves: Prep time:

Ingredients:

Method:

RECIPE

Serves:

Prep time:

Ingredients:

Method:

RECIPE

Serves: Prep time:

Ingredients:

Method:

RECIPE

Serves: Prep time:

Ingredients:

Method:

RECIPE

Serves: Prep time:

Ingredients:

Method:

RECIPE

Serves: Prep time:

Ingredients:

Method:

RECIPE

Serves: Prep time:

Ingredients:

Method:

RECIPE

Serves: Prep time:

Ingredients:

Method:

RECIPE

Serves: Prep time:

Ingredients:

Method:

RECIPE

Serves: Prep time:

Ingredients:

Method:

RECIPE

Serves: Prep time:

Ingredients:

Method:

RECIPE

Serves: Prep time:

Ingredients:

Method:

RECIPE

Serves: Prep time:

Ingredients:

Method:

RECIPE

Serves: Prep time:

Ingredients:

Method:

RECIPE

Serves: Prep time:

Ingredients:

Method:

RECIPE

Serves: Prep time:

Ingredients:

Method:

RECIPE

Serves: Prep time:

Ingredients:

Method:

RECIPE

Serves: Prep time:

Ingredients:

Method:

RECIPE

Serves:

Prep time:

Ingredients:

Method:

RECIPE

Serves: Prep time:

Ingredients:

Method:

RECIPE

Serves: Prep time:

Ingredients:

Method:

RECIPE

Serves:

Prep time:

Ingredients:

Method:

RECIPE

Serves: Prep time:

Ingredients:

Method:

RECIPE

Serves: Prep time:

Ingredients:

Method:

RECIPE

Serves: Prep time:

Ingredients:

Method:

RECIPE

Serves: Prep time:

Ingredients:

Method:

RECIPE

Serves: Prep time:

Ingredients:

Method:

RECIPE

Serves: Prep time:

Ingredients:

Method:

RECIPE

Serves: Prep time:

Ingredients:

Method:

RECIPE

Serves: Prep time:

Ingredients:

Method:

RECIPE

Serves:

Prep time:

Ingredients:

Method:

RECIPE

Serves: Prep time:

Ingredients:

Method:

RECIPE

Serves: Prep time:

Ingredients:

Method:

RECIPE

Serves: Prep time:

Ingredients:

Method:

RECIPE

Serves:

Prep time:

Ingredients:

Method:

RECIPE

Serves: Prep time:

Ingredients:

Method:

RECIPE

Serves:

Prep time:

Ingredients:

Method:

RECIPE

Serves: Prep time:

Ingredients:

Method:

RECIPE

Serves:

Prep time:

Ingredients:

Method:

RECIPE

Serves:

Prep time:

Ingredients:

Method:

RECIPE

Serves:

Prep time:

Ingredients:

Method:

RECIPE

Serves: Prep time:

Ingredients:

Method:

RECIPE

Serves: Prep time:

Ingredients:

Method:

RECIPE

Serves: Prep time:

Ingredients:

Method:

RECIPE

Serves: Prep time:

Ingredients:

Method:

RECIPE

Serves: Prep time:

Ingredients:

Method:

RECIPE

Serves: Prep time:

Ingredients:

Method:

RECIPE

Serves: Prep time:

Ingredients:

Method:

RECIPE

Serves: Prep time:

Ingredients:

Method:

RECIPE

Serves: Prep time:

Ingredients:

Method:

RECIPE

Serves: Prep time:

Ingredients:

Method:

RECIPE

Serves: Prep time:

Ingredients:

Method:

RECIPE

Serves: Prep time:

Ingredients:

Method:

RECIPE

Serves:

Prep time:

Ingredients:

Method:

RECIPE

Serves:

Prep time:

Ingredients:

Method:

RECIPE

Serves: Prep time:

Ingredients:

Method:

RECIPE

Serves: Prep time:

Ingredients:

Method:

RECIPE

Serves: Prep time:

Ingredients:

Method:

RECIPE

Serves: Prep time:

Ingredients:

Method:

RECIPE

Serves: Prep time:

Ingredients:

Method:

RECIPE

Serves: Prep time:

Ingredients:

Method:

RECIPE

Serves: Prep time:

Ingredients:

Method:

RECIPE

Serves: Prep time:

Ingredients:

Method:

RECIPE

Serves: Prep time:

Ingredients:

Method:

RECIPE

Serves: Prep time:

Ingredients:

Method:

RECIPE

Serves: Prep time:

Ingredients:

Method:

RECIPE

Serves: Prep time:

Ingredients:

Method:

RECIPE

Serves: Prep time:

Ingredients:

Method:

RECIPE

Serves: Prep time:

Ingredients:

Method:

RECIPE

Serves:

Prep time:

Ingredients:

Method:

RECIPE

Serves: Prep time:

Ingredients:

Method:

RECIPE

Serves: Prep time:

Ingredients:

Method:

RECIPE

Serves: Prep time:

Ingredients:

Method:

RECIPE

Serves: Prep time:

Ingredients:

Method:

RECIPE

Serves: Prep time:

Ingredients:

Method:

RECIPE

Serves:

Prep time:

Ingredients:

Method:

RECIPE

Serves: Prep time:

Ingredients:

Method:

RECIPE

Serves: Prep time:

Ingredients:

Method:

RECIPE

Serves: Prep time:

Ingredients:

Method:

RECIPE

Serves:

Prep time:

Ingredients:

Method:

RECIPE

Serves: Prep time:

Ingredients:

Method:

RECIPE

Serves:

Prep time:

Ingredients:

Method:

First published in 2025 by New Holland Publishers
newhollandpublishers.com
ISBN 9781760795030